Footprints

AF070678

Footprints

Josep Lluís Mateo
Writings 2005–2020

PARK BOOKS

Introduction

Philip Ursprung

If art and architecture aim at increasing complexity, whereas science and engineering aim at reducing complexity, Josep Lluís Mateo holds a position in-between these two poles. He can reduce the complex relationship between sustainability and architecture to the elementary categories of Earth, Water, Air and Fire. And he can turn the seemingly simple topic of iconic architecture into a differentiated meditation on space, monumentality and history.

His writings offer the same mixture of robustness and lightness, certainty and doubt, that one finds in his buildings. On the one hand, this is a result of his practice as architecture critic and editor of *Quaderns* and, since then, as the author of numerous books, essays and lectures. On the other hand, it relates to his design method, which starts with concepts, narratives and language rather than forms, shapes or images.

As an editor and critic, Mateo is used to writing about the work of others. Unlike most of his peers, his writings even today do not serve as propaganda for his own buildings or thoughts. As a consequence, there is nothing dogmatic, apologetic or strategic in his texts. Just as his buildings sometimes give the impression that he himself commissioned them in order to figure out something that he needed to understand, his writings seemingly have no agenda. They are there to clarify his questions. They are motivated by what he does not know rather than by what he thinks he already knows.

The notion of the project, from the Latin *projectum* ('leaping forward'), is intimately related to the notion of the question. Mateo's beautiful sentence, 'I have always thought that the great teacher proposes a question whose relevance and approach makes all the answers excellent', sounds like a motto for his design, writing and teaching. The shared question, raised by Mateo, unites the teacher and the students, the writer and the reader, the builder and the inhabitant. It opens up the space and increases the freedom for everybody involved.

Like footprints, Mateo's writings are both simple and complex. They remind us that one is never the first and never the last. They offer orientation and give an example. And they are a pleasure to follow.

On Nature

Earth, Water, Air, Fire: The Four Elements and Architecture Today	08
Earth	10
Water	12
Air	14
Fire	16
Earthworks	18
Desert	24
Shelter	25
Islands	26
Balearic Islands	27

Earth, Water, Air, Fire: The Four Elements and Architecture Today

Whereas in our recent past the paradigm by which architecture was measured was the city, now, the collective reference surrounding our design activity is the *relation with nature.* [1]

Sustainability as an economic but also a moral and political argument is clearly a consensus in our societies. It is a frequently abstract, formless argument with religious overtones (appealing more to faith than to reason), utilizable in political verbalism and drifting easily towards engineering technocracy.

In this context, a vindication of the presence of the four elements (earth, water, air, fire), by means of which the pre-Socratic philosophers envisaged humankind's relation with nature, seems extremely useful to the discipline today.

1. The urban condition is now omnipresent. After Rossi and Koolhaas, a manifestation of the operational impracticability of nostalgia or delirium, the city appears as a second nature, the product of processes other than the purely architectural. To regard the city, too, as nature, is to confirm the argument put forward here.

The elements connect us to nature as a *physical* phenomenon that can be experienced with the senses and is therefore directly related to architecture, which, as we know, addresses the real construction of the world, the alchemic operation that turns concepts into material.

The elements save our activity from the pure mathematic abstraction on which technology is based.

Our activity, at a primitive, archaic but very present level, consists in modelling the earth to geometrize its surface or piercing it to build foundations, erecting walls and roofs that protect us from rain and snow, and using the energy of fire as light and heat that make the resulting space habitable.

In the present-day state of globalization, in which the identity-modernity equation is appearing in a new light, the elements reproduced in all cultures as an initial moment with which human construction activity is related form part of a general vocabulary of common arguments. Having ruled out modernization as the uncontrolled application of the tired old prototypes of the metropolis, the intelligent, sensible manipulation of the elements provides the basis for specific projects that are, at once, rooted and globally comprehensible.

Earth

The earth is our support, our base – the root that will, eventually, allow us to fly.

To speak of earth requires us to think about water, the slow force that moulds, cracks and bores it; that transforms and, sometimes, also weakens it.

It also requires us to think about air, empty space, the wind that moves over the surface of the earth's crust and which our buildings, extensions of that crust, channel or resist.

Speaking about the earth represents another form of encounter with the local. An encounter with the remains of the wreckage: bones (the transformation of the organic into inorganic), stones, old foundations, traces.

And an encounter with matter: red clay, yellow sand, grey pebbles in strata or masses.

Our work with earth consists in hollowing it out, boring into it, penetrating it. Guaranteeing the transfer of loads and fluids towards it, where they dissipate.

Vertical dimension: gravitational and spatial.

It also consists in moulding it, reorganizing the topography (introducing geometry), reinforcing it, cladding its surface.

Horizontal dimension: superficial and open.

The earth: the start and the end of architecture.

IMG. 01   Michael Heizer, *Double Negative*, 1969. Moapa Valley in Mormon Mesa, Nevada

Water

Formless: water adapts to the container.
Colourless.
Tasteless.
Odourless.
Constantly moving: instability, dynamic behaviour.
In its movement, it bores, it breaks, it moulds.

Change of state: liquid to solid, and, when frozen, an increase in volume. However, it is not only the consistency that changes, but also our relationship with it. An ice field, for instance, is a place connected to the end of the world, the end of life. It is a landscape of survival rather than a place to dwell. In its liquid form, conversely, it is the opposite: a synonym of pleasure, of holidays and the enjoyment of life.

Necessary to life.

IMG. 02   Eva Afuhs, *Wasser I* (Water I), photographic study, 1994–1998

Air

At a basic, primary level, our buildings rest (downwards) on the ground, on the earth, and extend (upwards) into the air, into the sky.

The earth satisfies the need for anchorage, and the air offers the possibility of expansion, opening up, taking off.

Air entails many interesting issues that architecture has to address. One is verticality, the connection with the sky, with the cosmos. Another is the presence of wind – a powerful horizontal force penetrating built structures, which are typically pulled down vertically by their weight due to the force of gravity.

The sky is also covered by clouds; gaseous, they respond to temperature, changing their consistency to become rain (liquid) or snow (solid).

If architecture is, ultimately, solid, we have to interact explicitly with the gaseous, kinetic conditions of the medium. We have to reflect on its consistency, over and above the need to protect and enclose. Overcoming the solidity, density and fixation typical of architecture in order to associate with lightness and gaseous evanescence is one of the arguments of our existence as architects, since being realistic sometimes means asking for the impossible.

Architecture not only protects, encloses, limits; sometimes, the solidity of the construction disappears and melts into the gaseous consistency of the air.

IMG. 03   Mellerhutte, Garmisch-Partenkirchen, Germany

Fire

'τὰ δὲ πάντα οἰακίζει κεραυνός'
'It is the thunderbolt that steers the course of all things.'

Heraclitus, *Fragment 64*, trans. John Burnet. (This quote was also pinned to the door of Martin Heidegger's hut in Todtnauberg)

The ancients saw fire as the primordial element, the origin of the formation of matter. In our field of architecture, fire is associated with energy, with the thermal adaptation needed to sustain human life, and for handling and producing the materials (iron, glass, food) that are fundamental for survival. Fire is a synonym for the flow of life, which architecture serves.

Generally, fire is connected to energy, light, purification, illumination, creation, destruction and metamorphosis. It is classically associated with the properties hot and dry, and, once people ignited the first fire and gathered around it, it came to signify overcoming the hostility of the environment and appropriating the natural givens for human needs.

As a synonym for humankind's transcendental powers, fire stands at the origin of warmth and light. However, if not properly tended to, its benign character can quickly become a dangerous and apocalyptic nightmare.

Ultimately, the fireplace is the centre of the house: the hearth, connected to the vertical movement of dancing flames and smoke.

Fire has no precise consistency, but its presence can actively transform matter into different states. Places of production where fire is active are truly impressive and magical. Out of a river of fire, all manners of shapes later materialize and solidify.

IMG. 04   Walter de Maria, *Lightning Field*, 1977. Catron County, New Mexico.

Earthworks

Take two of my projects, thirty years apart: a recent work and an early scheme; despite the time lapse between them and their very different contexts, they have much in common.

Ancient sites – earthworks – reveal ruins, medieval or Palaeolithic remains. We, the architects, always begin by disrupting the ground, sometimes quite violently so. Some primitive cultures, such as the Incas of the Andes, for whom Pachamama – Mother Earth – is a divinity, have a special ritual allowing the builders to ingratiate themselves with her before starting construction, before digging the foundations.

IMG. 05 — Facade of the Film Theatre on Espalter Street in Barcelona, 2013

IMG. 06 — Church Square from Fort Street in Ullastret, 1985

When I was approached in the early 1980s to work on the urban design of Ullastret, near Girona in northern Catalonia, a place of great archaeological and historical significance, it was a rural medieval village. It was not urbanized at all. Bare earth still formed the surface of public spaces, and the infrastructure (water, light, sewerage) was chaotic and rather precarious. My role was to 'urbanize' the village.

In Ullastret, in the country, where we had to pave the public space, we first had to regularize the random, irregular topography. This rationalized reconstruction of the hillside's geometry in relation to the movements of people and rainwater flowing over its surface was fundamental.

This operation, for me, was magical. As an inhabitant of a city from which the earth on which it stands disappeared from sight long ago, I wanted to undertake this operation of necessary modernization with a subtle, special approach, sensitive to the place and its voices. What interested me was true modernization that also appreciated the complex of remains: Roman, medieval and present-day fragments, which, with almost childlike interest, I gazed at in amazement.

IMG. 07   Church Square before the intervention in Ullastret, 1982
IMG. 08   Church Square after the intervention in Ullastret, 1985

The Filmoteca, the new headquarters for the Film Theatre of Catalonia, was to be built in Barcelona's Raval district, one of the oldest parts of the historic city centre. Here, it was not so much the earth that attracted me at first (my relation with it later prompted long, complex processes). What initially interested me were the socio-morphological connotations of the place: the old Chinese Quarter; the abject prostitution and constant wretchedness lasting centuries. It had also been the site of frequent fighting, of violent scenes from even the recent past. The square, for example, is named after Salvador Seguí, an anarchist who was killed there.

This dark, suffocating world, the subject of films, photography and thrillers, was the area where I was to intervene, thereby changing, modernizing it. As in the case of Ullastret, I wanted this change to be special, sensitive and in keeping with the telluric force of that which already existed. I did not want my passage through this place to be bland, mannered or standard, or me to be incapable of responding with the necessary energy; an unworthy antagonist.

IMG. 09　　Construction of foundations for the Film Theatre in Barcelona, 2007

The dense urban context of the Filmoteca meant that, when construction work started, it revealed foundations, old walls, settlements. Here, the objective was not to construct a surface as in Ullastret, but to build upwards, to generate a volume. A volume that would comprise walls, planes. The logic of the wall and its direct constructive expression, with the nails and iron bars inside it, are a fundamental part of its character. It was a matter, then, simply of adding one wall more to its ancient, dilapidated neighbours. In the old town of Barcelona, my building sets out to express itself as pure structure: no cladding, no finishes. The bare concrete beams-cum-walls that form the facades are highly varied, proving themselves family members of the dilapidated neighbouring walls, where plaster crumbles to reveal their original central mass.

IMG. 10　　Main facade of the Film Theatre on Salvador Seguí Square in Barcelona, 2013

In Ullastret, the surface of the newly geometric site had to be clad, its skin defined. Here, the idea – I would almost say the delirium – was for this horizontal cladding to always react to its direct environs, to the walls of the facades: no boundaries and no other internal logic than the one provided by the geometry of the topography beneath. The fragment was the rule. Ultimately, each square centimetre was a specific problem. A system cannot last very long in a medieval city, and working with pavement meant obeying the general urban logic, in this case fragmented and multiple.

IMG. 11/12   Detail of the meetings of the different pavings after the intervention in Ullastret
1985   2020

 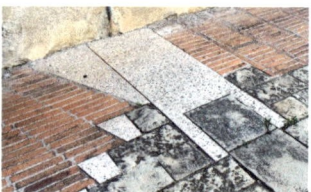

The Filmoteca is volume, not surface. It has inner space. Light is the protagonist. Light constructs movement, and accompanies it. The space is organized around two movements: the first is a descent into the darkness of the cinemas, with the reflection of the spectators (in turn reflected: actors seen in a series of mirrors). The second movement is an ascent towards the light, towards the places of work. The ascent from the foyer to the upper floors of the building is accompanied by natural light, introduced via a large skylight above the atrium where the escalators are located. Two such courtyards, connected but not continuous, accompany and orchestrate the movement.

IMG. 13   Entry of overhead light into the Film Theatre, Barcelona, 2013

But beneath all of this, in Ullastret and in Barcelona, it is the ruins that provide unity: Roman remains that formalize the planes of foundations and drains, and mark out the new structure of the buildings that follow. In time, walls are destroyed and roofs disappear. Only that which lies below the surface of things remains: those ancient earthworks on which new worlds are planned.

IMG. 14 Church Square under construction, Ullastret, 1983

IMG. 15 Archaeological remains found during excavations for the Film Theatre, Barcelona, 2007

Desert

'In a landscape where nothing officially exists (otherwise it would not be "desert"), absolutely anything becomes thinkable and may consequently happen.'

Reyner Banham, *Scenes in America Deserta*, 1982

To relate architecture to the desert is to imagine an object facing its antagonist, the zero degree of the exterior: infinite, extreme, mobile and endless.

It also means recalling architecture's properties of protection, of interior, of opposition to nature.

And that architecture, in its early days, called for the radical use of the resources available: a pole and some pieces of cloth (which we can take with us – you pass through the desert, you don't stay), a few stones we find, some worked clay.

Instruments of survival.

IMG. 16 Photograph by Reyner Banham of the Mojave Desert in California, 1980

Shelter

To speak of shelter is to recall an archaic, primitive aspect of our work. The condition of protection from a hostile exterior that marked the first steps of architecture's progress. We could then move on to the cave or the bunker as a manifestation of the will to survive. But continuing in the archaic atmosphere, I prefer to see it from another viewpoint.

> 'If the sedentary knows the value of things, the nomad [...] is acutely conscious of their fragility.'
> Titus Burckhardt, *Art of Islam*, 1976

In opposition to the rough, dark, solid, hard essence is the transparent, smooth, lightweight, open beginning.

And, as an initial shelter, I see Schindler House in West Hollywood, Los Angeles, built in 1921, as an outstanding example.

> Reyner Banham wrote that this house was built 'as if there had never been houses before'.
> Reyner Banham. 'The Master Builders: 5', *The Sunday Times Magazine* (8 August 1971).

Thick, prefabricated concrete walls are moulded into the ground to rise up vertically, exhibiting their bonds and profiles, slightly sloping. Strips of wood cover the spaces between them, generating Japanese membranes, as though made of rice paper.

The exterior counts. So, too, does the roof, with its open bedrooms.

The shelter is defined by an exterior that is open but close, controlled. Defined by lightness rather than thickness, by light rather than darkness.

Closer to the nomad's tent than the protective (thick-walled) enclosure of the farmer.

IMG. 17   RM Schindler Studio. Tilting a slab into place with block and tackle, 1922

Islands

'Rêver des îles, avec angoisse ou joie peu importe, c'est rêver qu'on se sépare, qu'on est déjà séparé, loin des continents, qu'on est seul et perdu – ou bien c'est rêver qu'on repart à zéro, qu'on recrée, qu'on recommence. [...] l'île, c'est aussi l'origine, l'origine radicale et absolue.'

'Dreaming of islands, whether with joy or in fear, is dreaming of pulling away, of being already separate, far from any continent, of being lost and alone – or it is dreaming of starting from scratch, recreating, beginning anew. [...] the island is also the origin, radical and absolute.'
Gilles Deleuze: 'Causes et raisons des îles désertes', 2002

Islands, finite, enclosed spaces: the limit as a condition and presence, as unifying moment. Small worlds in some cases extended by repetition: the archipelago, at times an architectural metaphor.

Islands traditionally raise two issues.

First, the priority of nature as an argument. On the continuous horizon of the sea, the figure unfolds with all the rhetoric of the landscape: mountains, rocks, trees, vegetation ... These will be the materials that construct the image.

Second, human presence in the activity of construction, until recently limited by possibilities (few) and impossibilities (plentiful). Examples of astuteness and symbiosis with the environment. Versions of the vernacular. In the past.

Now we have to add the transformation brought about by tourism and modernity. Cosmopolitanism versus endemism.

IMG. 18   Strombolicchio Island, Italy

Balearic Islands

My first encounter with the Balearic Islands came at a very early age, as a boy scout on an outing to Menorca. For me – a city boy, introverted but observant – that was the stuff of adventure: the journey on a dilapidated boat (the steamer *Mallorca*), an island with a special language, a history that was physically present (*talaiot* megaliths, castles, English sash windows), the sea and nature, a rural world.

A little later, Ibiza and Formentera appeared on the horizon. This was the romantic hippie world, which, from a distance, attracted me more than the pure political activism of the time – which was the other option for a restless young man.

Later still, I finally reached Mallorca, which I had never considered a possible destination, seeing it only as a place of mass tourism. I ended up in Sóller in a boat, after a very difficult six-day run from Castellón, with storms and engine failures, dead calm, etc. It was the Promised Land.

Making my way along the Serra de Tramuntana mountain range was amazing, and it marked the start of a long relationship which, when the moment came, I consolidated by building myself a house. Building is always an act of connecting with the earth, taking root. This we know.

Lots of things here interest me. One is the nature. I built my house in a place that is still scantly populated because the weather has always been extreme: wind from the north, storms, intense heat from the mountains in the south ... My house aims to provide at once shelter, protection and openness, contemplation of the spectacular exterior. Closing and opening at the same time. The sea and the sky meet in a line, with Cap de Formentor a blur in the background.[1]

Another central reason for my presence here is cultural. In the islands, and specifically in Mallorca, I found traces of the Mediterranean culture that is at the core of my identity. A culture that relates to a specific geography, with all that this implies of physical sensibility, and with the

Greco-Roman tradition that is superposed on other worlds: the presence of Arab culture and something unknown but real, prehistoric. In fact there is an archaism present in the local world which interests me.

My designs work on several fronts, but there is one that has always been an active component: a fascination with the primitive, archaic – let's call it the essential.

My house, which is highly abstract (another front that is not necessarily opposed to the others), is in dialogue with these themes.

The lattice wall built of *marés*[2] (I just had to use it!) draws the views and sculpts the light according to almost Berber patterns. I often retouch it, taking advantage of such a good material and the way it wears.

I always thought about my house in relation to the rocks, the geology, not in relation to the city or architecture.

It must be said that the place is hard, and I have to constantly strive to protect it.

[1] 'Josep Lluís Mateo ha construido una casa que se eleva, aparentemente indiferente a su entorno inmediato, y a la topografía local. En cambio, se concentra en el gran espectáculo del mar abierto, y el mundo que crea la propia casa.'

'Josep Lluis Mateo has built a house here that rises, apparently indifferent to its immediate surroundings and the local topography. It concentrates instead on the great spectacle of the open sea and the world created by the house itself.'
Excerpt from the text *La casa blu sul mare* written by Ignasi de Solà-Morales for the magazine *Domus*, no. 836 (April 2001).

2 Soft local sandstone, which is widely used on the island.

IMG. 19　　Lattice wall of sandstone blocks at the house in Mallorca, 2019

IMG. 20　　Sunset seen from the house in Mallorca during the summer of 2019

On the City

Volume, Void, Surface   32
Not Just Skin   34
Of Embodiment   36

Volume, Void, Surface

In the city, we define an urban space by means of the interrelation of objects in the *void*.

The *volumes* of these objects are unlikely to be the pure, platonic solids that Le Corbusier wrote about in *Vers une architecture (Toward an Architecture)*. Many different factors – brief, context, technology – will distort them, converting them into objects more like Brancusi's pieces; his studio a metaphor of the global city.

Basically, *surface* is a texture to be defined. In our case, we try to rediscover the earth, primeval nature.

The outer faces of the volumes present their enveloping surfaces. New textures appear. Despite Deleuze ('The deepest is the skin'), on occasions we have tried to see the skin as the expression of the bones, as a primitive invertebrate. Then, too, breaking it down into layers, going beyond the purely epithelial condition of its exterior to turn it into volume, into thickness.

IMG. 21 Atelier Brancusi, 11 Impasse Ronsin, 15e arrondissement, Paris, 1955

Not Just Skin

We were looking at the former Renault plant in Boulogne-Billancourt. It immediately brought to mind old stories of May 1968 and Jean-Luc Godard's film *Éloge de l'amour (In Praise of Love)* that was shot there shortly before the factory was demolished. However, when we visited the site, what we found was a huge, beautiful, expectant empty space, which involved constructing a new part of the city. As an architect, I like that sensation of emptiness waiting to be filled and taking on the responsibility of imposing clarity.

IMG. 22   Frame from the film *Éloge de l'amour*, by Jean-Luc Godard, 2001

This is a building designed in terms of volume and thickness, not just skin. The facades are structural concrete walls, which were a major technological challenge, but the kind of challenge a true constructor loves. The proportion and size of the openings were calculated in relation to the structural behaviour of the entire building. For reasons of energy efficiency, the walls, which I would have liked to have left bare, called for thick thermal insulation, which we then protected with aluminium sheeting. The side walls that continue the roof are made of zinc, a traditional artisan material that has a great urban tradition.

IMG. 23　Main facade of the LA FACTORY office building in Boulogne-Billancourt, Paris, 2010

Of Embodiment

An Interview with Josep Lluís Mateo
by Richard Scoffier

RS   You are currently in charge of Grand Central, the multimodal hub and business district in Nice. How do you see the relationship between architecture and urbanism?

JLM   There is of course a relationship, but they are not at all the same thing. The urbanist designs the general fit within the territory, focusing on questions of infrastructure (be they political-economic, social and ecological, as well as functional or circulatory).

The urbanist has to generate a set of general rules of play that define, for example, the urban space, clearly marked by the interaction between empty and full, between volumes and the space between them. They also have to articulate the interaction between the parts.

But urbanists should not try to define an architecture project from a bird's-eye view. On the contrary, they should provide the appropriate structure so that the project can express itself specifically in response to the concrete, to detail and material.

According to the Italian school, and particularly Aldo Rossi, we believed that we could design entire cities, create architecture by means of urban plans. That was a Postmodern moment of nostalgia for the enlightened power of the nineteenth century. But this is not the case! The role of the urbanist is not to design everything; it is to enable good architectures to emerge. I'm aware that 'good architecture' is a vague definition, but it's one I find useful. Good architecture is the vital germ of urban quality, a physical reality provided by architecture.

IMG. 24   *Occasional City* is an ideal city consisting of fragments of cities on which mateoarquitectura has been invited to work. The piece was shown in the exhibition *Footprints* at Galeria Joan Prats, Barcelona, in 2018

Between the historicist nostalgia of the unitary project of nineteenth-century enlightened power and the pure expression of the economic forces of today's neoliberalism (where the city as an interconnected project does not exist) lies the territory that I find interesting to traverse.

Let me stress once again the difference between these two profiles. One is more technocratic, and its mission is of general interest: to preserve unity, without which we would return to chaos. The other has to allow for the incubation of the city of tomorrow. But without good architecture, a good urban design project is simply not possible ...

The timescale of urbanism also involves difficulties. Soon, I will have been in Nice for eight years, and it is only now that the project is starting to take form, which is a little frustrating. In architecture, our relationship with time is already somewhat relaxed. We design projects that are carried out a couple of years later. But in urbanism, the timescales are even bigger.

RS   How would you define present-day urbanism?
JLM First there were urbanists, who were highly concerned with the economic side of space; then the architects who related to the morphology-typology dialectic; then those who celebrated chaos by anticipating the neoliberal city; and, finally, now we have the landscape architects, more sensitized to the ecological future of inhabited territories.

I'm not obsessed with the morphology of the street block, whether it should be open or closed; I don't think it's very important. I am, however, very interested in the appearance of ecological criteria, sustainability and primary relations with nature, firmly present on the contemporary scene.

I think they are symptomatic of the obsolescence of the stone city of the nineteenth century, of Haussmann's Paris or Cerdà's Barcelona. Those models of a regular, ordered city are tending to give way to a more territorial urbanism. We are seeing a shift from a totally artificial organization to more geographical planning: the nature of the land, the fauna and the flora ...

The traditional city was seen as an abstract social construct, independent of nature. Reintroducing interaction with nature into the urban discourse seems to me to be of great interest.

IMG. 25   Night view of the central axis of Grand Arénas, the new multimodal hub in Nice, France, 2018

IMG. 26   Climate diagrams for the Grand Arénas master plan for Nice, France, 2011–2018

Thermal comfort   Summer solar radiation   Natural ventilation – northwest wind

Values

Iconoclastia	42
Le Bon Sauvage	45
The Values of Architecture	48
Architecture, Next	51

Iconoclastia

In the past, buildings and other constructions representing singular moments in history for the community were called monuments. Their origin was an expression of power, a celebration of ritual or collective affirmation. They were normally solid; permanence was their rather unlikely objective. They were few, in a proportion of perhaps one to one hundred (a hundred being a more or less homogeneous continuous mass of dwellings and services, and one being the new and special object). Despite their limited number – or perhaps because of it – they tied the world around them together; they established relations with their surroundings (or forced others to). Definitely terrestrial, a monument was like a rock, like a mountain that rose up to dominate the plain.

The monument had an interior: the purpose of its thick walls was to protect what was seen as a sacred space. Within those walls, the boundaries of space were tattooed and made up; it was no longer the representation of construction that was offered, as on the outside. The walls were transformed into gold, the wood into pictorial representation; and light and, perhaps more importantly, dark marked what was to be seen and what, despite existing, went unseen.

In the contemporary world, a project that aspires to be exceptionally expressive (almost all of them) is commonly called an icon. The word icon, etymologically, signifies the representation of divinity by means of painting.

The abundance of Byzantine icons is well known; with their highly coded style, they were venerated as the presence of God and the saints on earth.

The presence of icons in contemporary architecture is defined by a series of characteristics that I would like to examine here.

One is multiplicity: in the contemporary city, everything is potentially iconic – that is, expressively autonomous, disconnected.

Walter Benjamin[1] wrote that the classical definition of the aura[2] of a work of art was the 'unique phenomenon of a distance', whereas the contemporary world changed the conditions of this phenomenon. Rather than 'distance', mass culture called for closeness, and for repetition rather than 'uniqueness'. In our case, iconicity may be seen to parallel repetition, copying and non-originality, and it is rarely related to closeness. Indeed, iconic buildings are ill equipped to deal with contact and close phenomenological analysis.

Icons do not guide, they do not create hierarchies; they declare their presence, but even though they may at a given moment impose it, that moment is fleeting. Sooner rather than later, new icons will appear and erase the earlier ones (or at least try to). The maker of icons, in his energetic, unceasing travels around the galaxy, does not tend to return to what in the past was a desert, the base on which the icon was built, now inhabited by new barbarian colleagues who perhaps reduce the effect imagined by its creator (or do they reinforce it?).

The place for the icon is a flat base and a backdrop. The desert is a suitable base, but water is still more highly prized: it reflects and reproduces the form. Since an icon is, almost exclusively, form, this multiplying effect intensifies its essence.

1. Walter Benjamin, *Das Kunstwerk im Zeitalter seiner technischen Reproduzierbarkeit: Drei Studien zur Kunstsoziologie* [The Work of Art in the Age of Mechanical Reproduction]. Frankfurt a. M.: Suhrkamp Verlag, 1981, p. 107.
2. The aura, in Byzantine iconography, is the circular halo around the head of a person represented, denoting their divine condition. The aura is used here to denote the special quality that separates everyday objects from those that are given particular artistic transcendence.

The place is also sky: blue, with clouds. It may incorporate – in its *renders*, as a sensitive adaptation to the place – a particular luminosity: more intense in Dubai, colder in Moscow.

The icon has no thickness; it is pure skin. It knows itself to be pure appearance and does not blend in. The skin must be spectacular in the sense of offering spectacle; night lighting is fundamental. Local motifs are always welcome: Gaudí in Barcelona, touches of feng shui in China, references to vernacular architecture (if there is any), etc.

The icon has no spaces, it has no interior. If an interior exists, it is of no interest.

Further, the icon frequently serves no purpose: the museum has no collection or the auditorium no orchestra. In this case, it is logical that acoustics simply should not exist.

The tradition of the icon includes its antagonist; the iconoclastic movement, which destroyed all representations of divinity, arguing that they destroyed its essence.

Le Bon Sauvage

> 'Gardez-vous de la pureté, c'est le vitriol de l'âme.'
> 'Beware of purity, it is the vitriol of the soul.'
> Michel Tournier, *Vendredi ou les limbes du Pacifique*, 1967

The imaginary of the profession of architect has historically seen the emergence of various paradigms. One, not too distant, is that of the globalized cosmopolitan genius, defending globalization and, to use its own terms, the generic, and constantly proposing new horizons, which he finds in Atlanta or in China. In the intellectual climate of the end of the last century, this professional figure emerged with its corresponding priests (I'm thinking of Rem Koolhaas) and a legion of, in many cases, less sophisticated figures who rushed greedily into the open marketplace where iconic personal style, faith in the extraterritorial goodness of technology (echoes of high-tech) or, simply, remains of mannered forms of modernity or classicism were applied.

The economic crisis at the beginning of this century and the widespread collective awareness of the devastation produced by this attitude have caused this line of – let's say cosmopolitan, globalizing – argument to lose its intellectual prestige. In more recent times, conversely, there is a great deal of data supporting the proposal of a new myth with a broad-based collective and media consensus.

Now, rather than the enlightened cosmopolitan, we find ourselves in the presence of – to use Rousseauian[1] terms – *le bon sauvage*, the noble savage.[2] Rousseau, openly at odds with the Age of Enlightenment of Voltaire's Encyclopaedists, defended the noble savage as the essence of truth and purity, an uncontaminated Emile in the natural world.

In our field, today's collectively active myths seem to be announcing similar processes.

As opposed to globalization, defence of the *local*. As opposed to cosmopolitanism, ruralism. The artist now lives in a *village*, preferably in an out-of-the-way place: up on a mountain, be it in the Alps or the Pyrenees. Or he appears to.

The noble savage is contemptuous of technology and, in his presumed withdrawal from the world, seems to distance himself from contemporary media and organization.

This character speaks little and, when he does, not always with rational arguments; he is comfortable with a kind of quasi-religious metaphysics. The favoured themes of his own particular system of saints are architecture as the conveyor of emotions, space as atmosphere, and nature as a primitive, acultural, essential reference.

Emotion, atmosphere, nature: themes that characterize this attitude.

Here, I would add *material*. The short-sighted view that this attitude proudly exhibits meets the physical world of the project and often takes it as a central argument. The object accentuates its material qualities, its close, tactile, sensible, central *presence*.[3]

The appearance of this figure, understandable historically as an alternative to previous proposals that are clearly no longer relevant, does not, in my opinion, conceal its weakness.

1. See Louis Althusser and Yves Vargas. *Cours sur Rousseau*. Paris: *Le Temps des Cerises*, 1972.
2. 'The myth of the noble savage was but a renewal and continuation of the myth of the Golden Age; that is, of the perfection of the beginning of things. The myth of the noble savage is the creation of a memory […].' Mircea Eliade. 'The Myth of the Noble Savage' in *Myths, Dreams and Mysteries*. New York: Harper & Row, 1975.
3. Hans Ulrich Gumbrecht. *Production of Presence: What Meaning Cannot Convey*. Palo Alto, CA: Stanford University Press, 2004.

A purported rural distance from the urban and global scene strips the proposal of the capacity to intervene anywhere other than in its own setting, the village. It presents us with an experience that is attractive, because it is archaic and engaging, but devoid of potential for development in broader horizons.

However, in a history such as ours where change, despite everything, is always the protagonist, new figures are probably already being announced for whom globalization does not oppose the local; intelligence and reason are shared values that serve to construct globally comprehensible languages and analyses; form has meaning, not just metaphysical value, and cosmopolitan openness is an effective instrument for the construction of the new.

The Values of Architecture

I have been asked to speak about values in architecture. This presents me with a twofold difficulty.

On the one hand, it is a very broad subject. This makes it difficult sometimes to advance with pure abstraction and easy to get bogged down by commonplaces.

On the other, we are faced with the difficulty, in the contemporary world, of finding general, commonly accepted values. Value is always a cultural and, therefore, social and historical phenomenon, which means it is in transition, changing.

While accepting the inevitable relativism, I will try to speak in terms of what is, obviously, my viewpoint, but with an approach that aspires to be broader, of more collective interest.

ARCHITECTURE AND SOCIETY

Architecture is the expression of the world. Without it, the world would be unintelligible. Our relationship with the social phenomenon, then, is direct and structural.

Architecture reflects and formalizes social energies, forces and passions without well-meaning idealisms: will to power, pettiness ...

However, the construction of a better world is the foundation, the lifeblood, of our profession, which is very much anchored in reality (necessarily) but aspires to broaden its perspectives, to build a new world. In our activity, it is difficult to imagine action as pure will that serves the continuation of the status quo. Among other things because, in this case, an architect would probably not be needed.

I think of our modern tradition: from the social hygiene movement in the nineteenth century that changed the typological conception of space, to the search for mass housing in the 1920s, with studies of the *Existenzminimum* or analyses of the internal functioning of the dwelling.

Our activity has always worked for the future, specifically for a better future.

The architecture–society relation is not deterministic, it is not based on cause and effect. Always, after the analysis, after the data, after popular participation, a project has to emerge. And this role of synthesizing data and determination to create a project, to produce a new reality, falls to architects; it is our role. If we do not accept it, others will (sociologists, geographers, politicians), because it is a necessary one. Analysis and accumulation of data do not automatically lead to a project.

ARCHITECTURE AS A PHYSICAL NARRATIVE

Architecture is directly related to the world of matter, of space, and of sensible experience. This brings us into contact with the world of science, but also with the world of sensations.

A project is always an idea, a dream that has to be controlled to make it reality.

Our work, as I see it, gravitates between two poles: one is ideal, utopian, abstract and pure; the other is material, raw and physical. This dialectic is typical of architecture and points to certain limits: pure political, ideological will, or pure manual sensibility.

SHARED VALUES

I referred earlier to the difficulty involved and the relativism that surrounds it. But in this context, I would like – with many provisos – to list some of the values that underlie our activity.

These common values are not the product of the present moment. They are old; they have always been there. They are the values that were first proposed by Vitruvius (the original theoretician of architecture) and then recalled by Alberti during the Renaissance.

And they are, still today:

Firmitas: the search for solidness, the value of matter, the importance of construction.

Utilitas: use, well-being, space. Architecture is not just surface or volume, it also has an interior. And, in this interior, human life plays out.

Venustas: the desire for beauty, transcendence, an instrument of connection and permanent communication of humankind.

On this basis, I think we can, with pride, defend our territory.

Which belongs to all of us.

Architecture, Next

Text written during the lockdown caused by Covid-19

1. Reflecting on the future from the perspective of the tough situation in which we currently find ourselves could set us off on all kinds of unattractive paths.

In an extreme form, these could be politically correct moralism or the reduced horizons of rediscovered localism.

I shall try to avoid them.

A first and obvious argument is *reflection on the development of globalization.*

And imagining the (perhaps naive?) possibility that the free movement of capital was controlled socially and had a positive influence on the general quality of life of human beings, it would and did not, as has been the case, represent the widening of the wealth gap and, with profit as the sole objective, the disappearance of the quality of things and life.

Also, that it was possible to imagine an interconnected world, where we could all fit together, rather than attending the familiar spectacle of the construction of walls and fortresses that separate and isolate us.

Some arguments that are closer to architecture:

2.	Faced with the emergence of digital technologies that we experience and use, *remember that architecture, our destiny, has the mission of building the real, physical world. The world of sensations, of space, of light, of matter. Increasingly necessary and important in a virtual world of pure ephemeral image.*

Of particular relevance in the future.

3.	It was my lot to live through the confinement and lockdown imposed by a pandemic in a remote place, with almost no human presence.

There, as spring arrived, I saw the prodigious unfolding of nature as it bloomed.

Nature, as the first reference point for architecture, an argument put forward at the same time by multiple places (ecology, engineering, sustainability ...), will certainly continue to grow.

Our architectural tradition can also proudly show how, at many moments in history, human construction activity has been based on an intelligent, non-predatory relationship with the natural setting. And how, by transforming the environment, it has helped it to develop.

Although it is perhaps a commonplace, the nature-architecture interaction will be – is – a priority argument in the future (to be avoided: political verbalism, economic cynicism, machinist excess).

4.	*Dominant ideas about the city have been affected by our recent experience.*

Both the myths of density and modernity's delusional growth, and nostalgia for the nineteenth-century historical city, are references to be reviewed. As is the mythology of public transport and its other side, the demise of the private car ...

We have to propose new urban models that, while guaranteeing interconnection and exchange, allow movement and enjoyment of collective space in safe, attractive conditions.

The discussion about new urban models has only just begun.

5.	Finally, this recent event – lockdown – has presented us with the direct experience of the *living conditions of our homes*. Unquestionably varied, with cultural diversities (such as differences in domestic space between northern and southern Europe), but in my opinion long in need of fresh ideas and proposals for this most important part of the built environment.

Excessively marked by the pure greed of capital and, at the same time, by the mental shutdown and operational rigidity of regulations and public systems of official control.

The consequences of this experience will probably be more visible in the mid- to long-term than immediately. And they will undoubtedly be the result of social agreements in which architects, as specialists in constructing new realities, have to provide necessary and appropriate syntheses (projects) for transformation.

Designing and Building

Designing and Building	56
Beginning/End	57
Gravity	58
About My Work	59

Designing and Building

Designing is an action that moves towards the future. It involves imagining another reality, another world, different from this one.

The project requires data about existing conditions: the place and its rumours, the use and its references, material and its conventions.

Yet the project distorts this data (and must do so): the place will (and must) be irremissibly changed, the use will evolve, it cannot be easily frozen, pacified, domesticated. The project will also distort the material or – even better – give it meaning: stone will be glass, or vice versa. The project will always reinvent, at least partially, the technology it employs.

The project as a necessary moment of invention looks to the future.

Building is a long journey through the present continuous. The past (the project) exists as an echo, as a phantasmal form that is no longer discussed, and sometimes even its origin is forgotten.

Building means taking root in the mud, squelching through it on a journey without distant horizons. We get used to short, sometimes microscopic distances. The present, detained and expanded, sometimes seems eternal, a place where I, at least, prefer to abandon any hope of transcendence.

Finally, the building appears. Despite the slowness of construction, suddenly the building is there. It is as though sustained effort over a long period of time is the initiatory condition that brings about its sudden appearance. And so we see it: whole, new, young, brilliant.

Very soon, we will leave it.

Beginning/End

Beginnings call for energy, joy, hope. They may seem like a game, and sometimes they must be precisely that.

Endings, now without hope of another possibility, call for blind energy without despair.

Endings require us to control our melancholy.

'Wenn man sich sein Haus fertig gebaut hat, merkt man, unversehens Etwas dabei gelernt zu haben, das man schlechterdings hätte wissen müssen, bevor man zu bauen – anfing.'

'When a man has finished building his house, he finds that he has learnt unawares something which he ought absolutely to have known before he – began to build.'
Friedrich Nietzsche, *Beyond Good and Evil*, 2009

The ending allows us, for a few seconds, to contemplate our work and, sometimes, to appreciate it.

The ending obliges us, immediately, to disappear, to abandon it to its fate. A necessary condition for our survival.

Gravity

The law of gravity is one of our themes. It speaks to us of the meeting with the earth, of being rooted, of solidness and of stability. Yet at the same time we also experience the opposing force: the will to fly, to float, to break free of our weight and conquer the air. Greek mythology offers us a beautiful description: Daedalus, the first architect and builder of the thick walls that enclosed the Labyrinth, was succeeded by his son, Icarus, who tried – and almost managed – to fly. We all know how that story ended. In my case, building walls (the definitive activity of an architect) is sometimes accompanied by the aim of making them levitate. I prefer to imagine covered spaces (building roofs) rather than constructing columns. The best column is one that is not there.

About My Work

My work speaks of places that I transform and continue.

Construction is a fight with time. Also, in such an artisan practice as mine, it roots us in a place.

I do not subscribe to the rhetoric of the noble savage. My work is nomadic; it speaks not so much of rootedness, of roots, of the earth. It is more of a hunter than a farmer.

My work speaks of space. In fact, one of the many things I have yet to do is something involving just space (no material, gravity or use), just floating space, with light and darkness.

I'd like my work to be cosmopolitan – understandable to everyone – without referring to my roots, without having to show them, or at least for them to be implicit, not explicit.

As I see it, in the world of globalization, the exalted, messianic turn-of-the-century discourses have not borne fruit; they are finished.

As are high-tech versions and epithelial mannerisms.

Historical discourses have shown their limits and their expiration date.

Nor do I recognize myself in the contemporary propositions of the noble savages: on the periphery, rooted, local, anti-urban, pseudo-Franciscan, their discourse conceals a lie, even though their work is intense and can indulge their materiality, which the close relation with the work allows.

I would like to take a third way: cosmopolitan but attentive, specific but understandable to everyone, close to the material but not bound by it, with roots but not showing them: we have to extend the field, not insist on its boundaries.

Teaching and Learning

Teaching Design	62
Building and Teaching Answers to an Architecture Student	66
	68

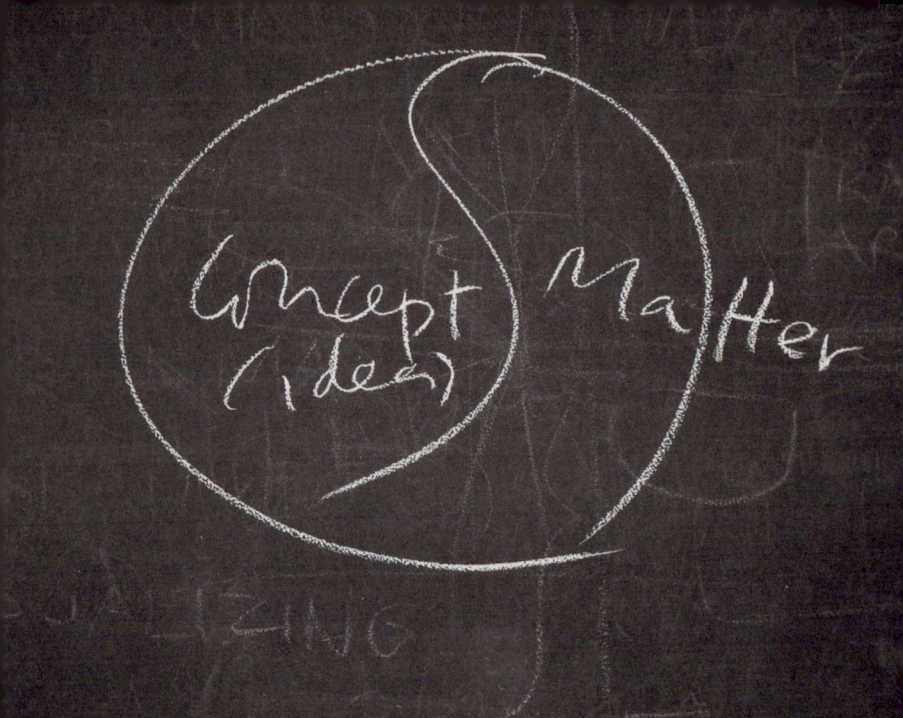

IMG. 27 Notes on a board by Josep Lluís Mateo

Teaching Design

IDEA AND MATTER

Our mission is to teach students how to design; that is, to imagine in physical terms a new reality and to be able to make it possible – to build it.

My interest is more conceptual – that is, abstract – than stylistic or formal, and always based on the awareness that we, the teachers, pose the questions and the students should produce the answers. I have always thought that the great teacher proposes a question whose relevance and approach make all the answers excellent.

As I see it, the practice of architecture gravitates around the idea–material dialectic. In architecture, these two terms are intrinsically interrelated in a very specific way. Our students are then faced as of day one with the task of introducing the thickness of material into ideal abstraction, using the logic of the supporting structure as the principle of order for the project, or imagining light as a material for constructing space: relating the physical world of sensible experience with the abstraction of the idea.

In this process, what interests me is the need for both pragmatic coldness and the fire that emanates from its apparent opposite: the anticipatory delirium of those who construct the future. Without this fire, the architecture loses value.

One of the things that is possible, albeit difficult, for the teacher to transmit is enthusiasm, a vital interest in knowledge and discovery.

That is what we try to do.

DATA AND INSTRUMENTS

The project materializes thanks to a great multiplicity of previous data. Data about its surroundings, its context and, therefore, a degree of controlled amplification of the field is always attractive. The city, nature, specific cultures are data around which the project discourse is constructed. There is also internal data that corresponds to the use, to the function that the project is to host and transform into space or into economic and technical feasibility. Data.

Observation and analysis in the *search for a project* are attitudes that can be transmitted and learned, and, in our own field, there are also instruments that we use to operate, which can and must be learned.

We have to use *images* to stage a new imagined reality, a fiction which, in our hands, will – this is the promise – become the everyday setting for our exterior: others. Images are also instruments of dialogue with our interlocutors.

Models allow us to analyse both volume and space, and we have to become practised in seeing their possibilities, scales and consistencies.

Alongside analysis, project culture is the culture of action and therefore entails constructing new events. Insisting on instruments also means insisting on the factual, productive side of design activity.

DISCOVERING AND SHARING

Learning, acquiring knowledge, means increasing our state of awareness, incorporating into our baggage arguments, references and forms that were previously unknown to us.

The metaphor of a person jumping is a good one. The jumper runs, takes the ground (what he knows) as his base and projects himself upwards, flies and lands somewhere unknown.

The project as an instrument of knowledge, certainly, but most of all as an inventive activity that transforms data into something that is at once appropriate, evident and unusual, and new.

Our task is often to prompt this leap. To remove the certainties, the commonplaces, the coarseness of what the students know, obliging them, alone and stripped bare, to produce something new.

Despite certain limitations, teaching project design has something in common with research. It is a place where data necessarily provides the basis for the production of quanta of new personal and sometimes collective knowledge.

Although our action as designers has to be intense and very specifically targeted, our mind also has to operate with a breadth of vision and categories. We have to be on the ground, squelching in the mud and fighting for each detail, and, at the same time, we have to be able to fly in order to gain an overview.

The teaching experience, once analysed, reviewed and extended, will produce texts and materials that will be made available. Teaching is not just the ineffable moment of coming together of teacher and student.

Sharing is the other side of discovering.

Building and Teaching

An Interview with Josep Lluís Mateo
by Isabel Concheiro and Anna Hotz

IC & AH   Could you talk about the relationship between your academic activity and your professional practice? In what way do they influence each other?

JLM   I consider myself a professional architect. Having said that, I have to point out that this has not always been the case. At the start of my career as an architect, it was not clear what I was going to do. In fact, I spent some years as a critic, editor and publisher. At the end of that period, I discovered that the most exciting part of this job was being a real architect, building and engaging in action.

However, I have always found the space outside of practice both thought-provoking and exciting. It is obvious that I am not going to teach my way of designing; I never try to reflect my work in this field. What is interesting to me as a teacher is the fact that we share a space where we are faced with a problem that has no clear answer. What is interesting is thinking, and teaching how to think. What are the questions? What are the fields? What are the arguments in the discipline? For all of us. If there is interaction between the two activities, it is the possibility of thinking about architecture without being forced to produce it. You can therefore be analytical, see different possibilities and even appreciate vastly differing positions. I always try not to have any personal solution to the problem, just analytical tools. And also to ask for synthesis in a high-quality result.

IC & AH   Today, in the academic and the professional world, we are faced with a dialectic relationship between the specificity of the local and the genericness of the global. How do you address this dialectic in your teaching?

JLM My presence here at the ETH Zurich is, to some extent, an expression of this dialectic. Part of the European identity is built on a north–south dialectic.

Ultimately, we must be open to understanding and appreciating things, even if they are not our own. The scientific side of the profession is a kind of cultural clash – load path, refraction and structural diagrams all speak a common language and make a collective argument.

We therefore have to be open and flexible, but we also need a solid set of instruments with which to operate. And this is something that we have to convey to our students.

In today's globalized world, we all have our origins and our traditions; they are a departure point but they cannot be the destination. Increasingly, we are starting out from different positions and coming together in shared projects.

IC & AH What, generally speaking, is the role of academia in the production of knowledge?
JLM Academia is a term from the eighteenth and nineteenth centuries. The academics were the enemies of the moderns. Academia was conceived as something apart from life, apart from contemporary, necessary things, concerned only with power and position. Academic knowledge is, in a way, an expression of knowledge without life or energy, purely archaeological and with no practical application.

The present-day version of academia would be more infrastructural: constructing a place at the right moment, with the right people, so that the interaction generates knowledge. The Architectural Association in the 1960s was an interesting place that produced a whole constellation of characters who have gone on to become references of the architecture of our time.

The present-day version of this scenario – though not very common – also exists. Places where the adventure of knowledge takes place and brings together a heterogeneous community of qualified actors, whose interaction generates lines of analysis and action that build the new project that is needed.

Here, I think we are in one of those few places.

Answers to an Architecture Student

*An Interview with Josep Lluís Mateo
by Piotr Lopatka*

PL   Synthetic and linear thinking: how can we do both?
JLM   Action (because the project is a proposition to act, to do something) is the product of synthetic thinking.

Analysis is the product of processes that are more linear or even meandering (not precisely one thing after the other). The analyses try to understand something, not precisely do something.

We need to be able to analyse the world freely and openly.

But we must not get lost in analysis. As architects, we have to be ready to produce a synthesis (our own, one that is personal but also has to be collective): a project in which we believe, which we are ready to build, considering another form of negotiation with reality. Creative and destructive at the same time.

(Destruction and creation are two sides of the same coin, remember!)

PL   Do we learn architecture by reading words or by reading images?
JLM   Words are a means to communicate, to express abstract thinking. Forms are the physical expression of the world and ideas.

Personally, I have always hated architecture that only relates to forms; it can easily end in pure ornamentation or sentimentalism. I prefer the energy of ideas, trusting that the form will follow.

Having said that, we have to learn, enjoy, experience and understand the material logic of our reality. This includes the composition of the landscape, the different ways that materials react in our hands or the magical nuances of light in space. We also have to refine our senses into a single specific thread ...

PL   Do urban artefacts have a poetic interior?
JLM   Not always. In many cases – especially in our cities, which are basically made up of housing – the urban artefact is fundamentally a screen or a skin with volume.

Domesticity, of course, doesn't produce epic spaces. It is – and has to be – more connected with privacy and direct contact with the senses.

But on the other hand, the truly urban architecture that I remember does have space: the Pantheon in Rome is unbelievable. The church of Santa Maria del Mar in Barcelona and the cathedral in Palma de Mallorca, both purely urban spaces, have a collective as well as a personal poetic ... So we have to fight to create spaces, even today.

PL   Does architecture produce just one image (neither interior nor exterior)?
JLM   I understand where your question is coming from. It depends on the point of view. You can be metaphysical, abstract, essentialist or reductive; and classicism and minimalism produced these practices. A single thing, with everything there.

Personally, I am more interested in multiplicity – the possibility of adapting and expressing the complexity of life today. I don't want to go to baroque extremes, but I do prefer to be able to consider everything.

PL   How important is the process?
JLM   The process is important, of course, but what really matters is the finished product: the building; it has to speak for itself. The importance of the process lies in its role in producing the best possible building, and this calls for intelligence, patience and energy. Architects are the only agents needed throughout the entire process with a goal to achieve, a project to do. The process, the way we do something, is judged by the end result.

And that, sometimes, can be a drama.

Dialogues

Origins – with Philip Ursprung	72
Resistance – with Fredy Massad and Alicia Guerrero	80
Constant Turning Point – with Félix Arranz and Jaume Prat	88

Origins

An Interview with Josep Lluís Mateo
by Philip Ursprung

PU   Could you tell me about your childhood and your family situation?

JLM   As I remember it, I was very introverted and very much a loner as a child, one who observed the world with a certain perplexity and with eyes wide open.

My father started out wanting to be an architect. At that time (in the late 1920s), architectural studies began with two years of mathematics followed by extremely hard exams in drawing. If you passed, you got admitted into architecture school. My father, whom I have very fond memories of, passed the entrance exam and continued studying both subjects. He finished the exact sciences quickly, just before the beginning of the Spanish Civil War.

After the war, during which he fought on the Republican side, he passed the exams for the post of Professor at the School of Engineering of Terrassa, which meant that the family had to move to Barcelona. That also allowed him to get his degree in architecture a few years later, but by then he was already working in the field of engineering. I was born around that time, and as a result of this situation, which was undoubtedly frustrating and hard for him, it was decided that I should be an architect, and I was given an architect's education already during my childhood. It was, on his part, a sort of deferred revenge on fate: someone who had not had the chance creating the ideal learning conditions for another.

In our house, there was a large library. I was always surrounded by books and I – like I said, always an introvert and a loner, especially as a child – used them, as the Barcelonan poet Jaime Gil de Biedma put it, to 'imagine certainties and cure wounds'. In any case, I remember when I was very small, along with my comic books, looking at very elementary books on Gaudí, Le Corbusier and Mies.

PU   What was it like growing up in Barcelona in the 1950s and 1960s? What marked you the most?

JLM   I was born in the Eixample, very close to Gaudí's building La Pedrera. When we moved to the northern part of the city in the late 1950s, I was a witness to the construction of this new area. In those years, the development of the city occurred in a sort of organic and metastatic process: it just grew and grew. I remember being surrounded by building sites and new buildings. From my house, you could still see rural areas. Within a few years they'd become part of the city, with modern buildings by architects like José Antonio Coderch and Francesc Mitjans.

In fact, the architecture of the 1950s left works of great interest everywhere, and in Barcelona as well. Some of the best local examples are in the area where I grew up.

PU   It was the time of the Franco dictatorship. Was it difficult to travel?

JLM   Yes, for both financial and political reasons.

My first trip was to Paris, when I was eighteen. In the Barcelona of the time, Paris was the place to be. French was the second language taught in schools, so Paris was a natural choice. After that I took long trips every summer. I hitchhiked, usually on my own. I went on a long trip to Scandinavia and Finland, where I was more impressed with Arne Jacobsen than with Alvar Aalto. Another summer I crossed Europe. I went to Prague. From there I went to Athens and returned via Italy. I stopped off in Ithaca, following Ulysses' route. I realized that it was the same landscape, the same sea and the same sun as in Barcelona.

For a young man living under the Franco dictatorship, those long journeys felt extremely romantic and adventurous. They also heightened my feeling of alienation. In fact it wasn't until much later that I realized that I was, that I wanted to be, from here.

I went to America much later, when I was thirty. But I have always identified more with Europe.

PU	Did you always want to be an architect?
JLM	In the context that I was brought up in, it was taken for granted that I would be an architect. Maybe that's why I had serious doubts. However, there was no obvious alternative. I didn't have any other clear choice. I found I was good at maths and science, and that I was interested in the humanities: art, culture, sociology, and the disciplines that help you understand the world. Engineering studies in general struck me as being limited, but in architecture I wasn't at all interested in the artisan component, as I saw it: drawing, models ... all that sort of epithelial craftwork.

In the end I studied architecture in Barcelona (at the only school at the time) from 1967 to 1973, but I had considerable doubts about my future.

PU	Which architects did you admire?
JLM	During my student days, which is when you discover the pleasure of the feeling of acquiring knowledge, the most interesting to me was Archigram. I also liked New Brutalism projects. I was impressed by the critic Reyner Banham. I remember *The Architecture of Four Ecologies* (1971), without doubt a fundamental book for defining the myth of Los Angeles, and a lot of others that I found in my father's library. I liked the Smithsons, James Stirling's work at the time, Candilis-Josic-Woods (their project for the Free University of Berlin, the African projects, etc.), Yona Friedman. Their positions were utterly opposed to the local culture that I lived in, where the debate was limited to craftsmanship, tradition and bricks. I was from another world. My alienation also had to do with this.

PU   Did you ever think about being a writer?

JLM   My father died in 1973, just as I finished my studies. All of a sudden I had to be an adult. I spent years closing down my father's studio, supervising works, finishing projects that I hadn't started, and I invested a great deal of effort in it.

But I needed to know more, broaden my horizons, learn. That's why I started to work as a critic. I had always learnt from books, and one writes because one reads. In times of hardship I might have thought of dedicating myself exclusively to writing, but at that time I also enjoyed the energy and pleasure of building, that collective force in which the architect can play an interesting role. I am an architect because I build. Without the building part, I'm not interested in this job at all.

PU   Which writers and theoreticians interested you?

JLM   My education was extremely classical. I have always been attracted to people who combine theory and practice, and I am very interested in thought linked to action. I read a lot by poets and artists who also theorized, for example the writings of Charles Baudelaire, Eugène Delacroix's *Journal* and T. S. Eliot. Along with this close-up criticism, I was also interested in German and Austrian art historians, such as Aby Warburg, Erwin Panofsky and Ernst Gombrich. They used their distance from their subject intelligently, with a mix of general knowledge and passion.

What I found contemptible was the solely political role of the critic, using his arguments without any interest in the subject analysed, practically immune to it. The Tafurian school, of which I had plenty of examples around me in Spain, was a clear example of ideological discourse without any interest in the work.

PU   I visited Barcelona for the first time in 1987. I remember that the port was still a dark, dense place, and it was dangerous to go into the old part of the city. When I returned in the mid-1990s, it was all safe, and the city looked much like other big cities.

It had lost something: part of its history, its past, which had been suppressed, it had disappeared. But when I visited the Joan Güell Multifunctional Complex, the suppressed was once again present. The enormous underground parking garage and the odd details in the marble pavement made me think that I was about to embark on an archaeological expedition. Can you tell me something about your concept of history?

JLM   I'm very interested in the relationship between history and archaeology. One of my childhood dreams was to be an archaeologist. I was fascinated by their work: discovering fragments, putting them back together, analysing the manifold layers of an object without having a clear idea of the whole. Freud mentions the idea of an 'archaeology of the mind' as a metaphor for the cognitive process. For me it is still an interesting metaphor. I'm not interested in what lies beyond history. I am somewhat indifferent to the contemporary. But I love the ancient, such as, for example, prehistoric ruins. I think about history and reality without really distinguishing between the old and the new. And I don't feel any sort of sentimentalism towards history or the past. Even modernity is history. Mies's buildings are already a century old.

PU   Two projects that I like very much are a work that was never built for the Lustgarten in Berlin (1994) and the new offices of the Deutsche Bundesbank in Chemnitz, currently under construction. Both are in the former German Democratic Republic. Was the demise of the GDR an important issue for you?

JLM   Not really. But I've also been surrounded by German culture, starting once again with my father, who spoke German: in his library, he had the original writings of Albert Einstein and Heinrich Wölfflin, which I obviously did not understand, though they did have a certain incomprehensible, if fundamental, value – mythical, cabalistic and arcane.

I visited Germany for the first time in 1986. Hans Kollhoff invited me to a summer academy. Marcel Meili was there, as was Jacques Herzog, among others. I lived in Berlin for a few months. It was the time of Wim Wenders's film *Wings of Desire*. There I discovered that the new united Europe was to entail the meeting of two traditions, the Catholic and the Protestant, and that north and south were going to produce a new synthesis, a point of encounter which I am still attempting to move towards.

PU   In addition to site and history, the theme of time – or rather a sense of time – seems important in your projects. On the one hand, there is a sort of narrative plot in each project; each one seems to tell a story. On the other hand, they inevitably speak of the setting. How does your design process work?

JLM   Yes, a project always tells the story of a specific place and time. A story that many still don't know but expect to be told.

Almost all my works stem from competitions. Winning a competition – when it's not rigged – means that many different people grasp an idea, it interests them and they support it: they adopt it as their own. And this happens when that story, which is made up, is at the same time real. The project announces a world that, although it does not yet exist, is latent.

You ask me about the process. Building – my ultimate goal – is a long road with different stages. There is an initial moment of invention and design. This is fundamental. There are specific materials and tools to work with. This should happen quickly. You might spend a lifetime getting this far, but in the end the creative act has to be quick. Then comes the time to build. This period can be very long. As a builder, you need certain virtues, such as perseverance, patience, passion and constancy. Nietzsche added another basic feature: the melancholic nature of builders. Melancholic because, in the building process, they always find they have learned something that they should have known from the beginning. The building process is a very important time period.

This profession continues to interest me due to the possibility of solidifying a kind of social ambition. To make solid something that is not. If not, it would melt into the air, as Marx said. An alchemical process occurs.

I love the physical aspect of building and the physical part of the intellectual work. And, in-between, there's a third period: the stage at which the project progressively takes shape, while it is being discussed. I try to follow it without getting burnt out.

PU	You became known internationally with the urban renewal of the town of Ullastret (1985). In that project, it seems that you framed and organized the existing buildings rather than restoring, and thereby eliminating, them. It's as though Walker Evans had been walking around the town guided by Carlo Scarpa, but offering photos instead of taking them. Can you explain something about your interest in painting, images and photos?

JLM	I love that image of Walter Evans with Scarpa in Ullastret. It's very fitting.

At some point, you realize that taking a photo is like doing a project. You define a certain reality with a certain quality. Interesting photos transform the object, or the view of the object, without destroying it. You complement something in a new way. Perhaps you grasp something you hadn't seen before. At the same time, it's a characteristic cultural intervention: to see something that no one has seen before, something which was, nonetheless, there all along. Photography has contributed to this remodelling and reorganization of reality, of that same reality, without destroying it.

It was a very attractive theme for me, a means of escape from the utopian projects of the 1960s that I came of age with. In the 1960s, personal revolution and vitalism combined with the Maoist and anti-Franco movements. In both, personal or collective utopia was the ultimate horizon. Later, there was a sort of common agreement, once again associated with my generation, that the existing reality was much more powerful than any utopian dream. Reality, even when it was dirty and marginal, was much more exciting than any fantasy of a better world. Photography as a tool was closely linked to the creation of a new reality, associated with an existing reality.

    I had a lot of friends who were photographers. But after a time I realized that this sort of photographic approach wasn't enough. The true task of the architect is to change reality. I was aware that photographers make lovely, decadent photos in the style of Walker Evans in which they show the dirt and marginal areas in a special light. But in the end, the architect is on the enemy's side, on the side of those who destroy all of it and then build something new: clean, shiny and obscenely polished. Once I realized that, the contemporary marginal romantic landscape lost some of its attraction.

    It is increasingly difficult to produce a photo, and increasingly difficult to write. After some time, I decided it was too much. I want to produce not photogenic buildings, but real buildings, good ones. That's what I do. Others will have to concern themselves with the transformation. Others will have to carry out those interventions, transforming the three-dimensional object into a flat experience in black and white or in colour. This practice is very important, since it has to do with mediation. It's like being a critic; a critic lends meaning and aura to something. But when I realized that my job was simply to construct objects, I gave up on constructing the description. It's better for my work. It's better if it's considered independently.

Resistance

*An Interview with Josep Lluís Mateo
by Fredy Massad and Alicia Guerrero*

Almost ten years after this conversation with Josep Lluís Mateo, and rereading it in the context of the present – on the delicate tightrope we walk today – I find his words imbued with a renewed, reaffirmed validity. At one point in this dialogue, he referred to Walter Benjamin's Angel of History and to the twists and turns, and the confluences of the past, present and future. The scenario in which we talked then was one of a time of uncertainty, marked by the consequences of major economic recession, which seemed to lead inexorably to a transformation of ways of understanding architecture: an obligation to look directly, from the foundering present left by the ravages of that crisis, towards a still insubstantial future. For me, a conversation with Josep Lluís Mateo has always been a lucid provocation to review and reinterpret my sense and vision of the present, and to understand the positive potential and forces that the past and the future contain for it. Returning today to this conversation means finding resistant ideas – ideas for resistance – on the basis of which to sustain vital and urgent paths of reflection and criticism.

IMG. 28   Paul Klee, *Angelus Novus* (New Angel), monoprint, 1920

FM & AG Your exploration of the concept of globalization a decade ago seemed to adopt a distance from the predominant stance of the time, correctly anticipating some of the risks that it implied.[1] Now, faced with the failure of an idea of global architecture as capricious decontextualized objectualism and the collapse of the 'black holes of globalization' you referred to back then, together with the serious ethical doubts surrounding globalizing projects constructed in China and Dubai, how do you think we can reconsider the idea of globalization?

JLM Architecture is a phenomenon that – despite being linked to the earth and very local in nature – has an abstract component that makes it more generalizable; it has always had a global dimension. Throughout history, there have been movements that have made their way around the world, with architectures that can be seen to be connected.

But these questions surrounding globalization, situated in the specific context of the time when I formulated them, have to be interpreted as an attempt to distance myself from Kenneth Frampton's theories of critical regionalism, which seemed very limited; I saw something a little outdated in them that was not very appealing. They were like formulations that would discover a strange 'noble savage', unable to survive being transferred to civilization for want of resources to be able to relate to the contemporary world.

While historically architecture has had a meta-territorial component, the present-day phenomenon of globalization is undeniably much more complex and has substantially undermined the bases of what I was interested in seeing as architecture; though, at the same time, I think that the phenomenon of globalization is inevitable.

Any theorizing about globalization that aims to be operative has to understand the evident fact that the

---

1. See Albert Ferré (ed.), *Josep Lluís Mateo, Textos instrumentales*, Barcelona: Gustavo Gili, 2007, chapter 'Especificidad', pp. 50–69.

presence, strength and energy of this phenomenon is driving us towards a world in which our messages can be heard by everyone, irrespective of the geographical point from which they are emitted, and this allows us to aspire to a more interconnected culture.

But, at the same time, my stance set out to oppose readings of globalization which, as I saw it, represented the disappearance of architecture in terms of an intellectual, creative and socially useful activity; as an expression of the world that constructs places and spaces intelligently, fittingly, beautifully. And the perversion of this essential question, turning it into a mask – frequently a ridiculous one – has been the negative face of globalization.

To some extent, these lines of action have been highly effective and have facilitated construction at a rapid pace in many parts of the world, but they have also demonstrated that architecture can be a very destructive activity. Construction, by definition, is always an aggressive act, and for me that is a crucial fact. We might say, to some extent, that when you build something many things die. For better or for worse.

I have seen nothing positive in this implantation of alien buildings, understanding this architecture to be absolutely related with the financial bubble. It is not just a moral or aesthetic argument that has put an end to it, but the conditions of today's reality and the extremely serious economic consequences that these buildings have had. Many of the countries where growth has been particularly strong implemented lines of action to bring about the destruction of architecture. They did not lead to development, but instead became a kind of pathology.

FM & AG   If we had not reached a situation of economic crisis, we would still be immersed in sham and pomp. The fact is that the crisis was long foretold, but we didn't understand until we saw the evidence for ourselves. What do you consider to be a truly efficient model of architect for the times we are living in, which call for precise reconsideration, changes in attitude and new stances on action?

JLM An individual who is informed, who makes an effort to understand a problem and who analyses, debates and proposes in an attempt to synthesize the forces at play (natural, economic, social, etc.); one who, given the intense effort required by any project, is a trusted collaborator for the client; this is the model of an architect I am most interested in being and one that I think represents a more contemporary concept. This is the model I consider to have a present. The phenomenon of the architectural star system and godlike architects on pedestals is no longer relevant today.

FM & AG In an article written in 1984[2] you called for criticism to go hand-in-hand with action: a kind of criticism that stimulates intellectual tension and emotional contact with architecture and truly interacts with architectural creation. The situation of criticism today is far more worrying than the state reflected in that article: the excessive intellectualization of postmodernity and the discourses introduced by technological changes in the early 1990s have given way to the vain, vacuous discourse and rhetoric of hypercapitalism and conceptualizations that seek to justify and legitimize architecture as object.

JLM My view may be rather old-fashioned, but I think that criticism has gradually become a kind of instrument for promotion.

These days, there is no discussion of values: they are either broadcast or sold. It is the power of the architect or client rather than the truth or judiciousness of a theory that sets the criterion of value. The direct use of discourse in vacuous messages (they surround us today, try as we might to ignore them) to justify something that has nothing to do with the building only serves slowly to undermine the force of the message.

2. "La necesidad de la crítica" in Albert Ferré (ed.), *op. cit.*, pp. 31–32.

The Internet has seen a radical change in the mechanisms of written systems, culminating in the disappearance of the foremost figures who were unquestionable intellectual authorities speaking out from a central point. The Internet allows the more direct appearance of new messages alongside the disappearance of this more central point of influence. There is a multiplicity of voices today, but many have no interest whatsoever in architecture, and lots of people realize they are not worth listening to.

In the long term, this situation may change, but at present the traditional role of criticism as a mediator between a message and an audience, between a creator and an audience, or as the dissemination and analytical definition of issues and situations has disappeared.

FM & AG   The construction of a pavilion for the National Museum in Prague is expected to be completed in 2012. How does this relate to the small scale?

JLM   The small scale is absolutely necessary for some things. Local architecture is often discredited when it gives up pretension in order to concentrate on small constructive details, but the materialization of architecture sometimes needs this great precision. Sometimes it is a much more general aspect – a detail that is repeated, a one-off decision that is then extended. But there are times when a one-off decision is just that, and there is no system, or only a very small system.

In the generic architectures of globalization we were talking about earlier, the lack of attention to detail is obvious. You can feel the absence of specific thought, something produced by a very distant viewpoint that doesn't understand the implicit nuances that exist between a corner, a wall or a stairway, that doesn't understand that there is a whole world needing to be followed and formalized, given expression. That is why this short distance is necessary; it is not always indispensable, but we have to recognize and be able to resist it.

FM & AG At a complex moment of transition, how do you assess your career, and where do you see the way forward today without giving in to unconscious or fainthearted escape clauses?

JLM When I look at the present and at architecture, my discourse is not – cannot be – negative. Despite all the traumatic signs of change, I think that architecture as an activity and a need will continue to exist. We will have to adapt, something that architects have always done.

The architect has always been a figure floating among many things, and this for me is one of the attractions of this profession. I've had some very difficult moments. I've been an architect, but I've been able to be other things; occasionally, I've thought I could have been a writer, a critic or a publisher. But having experienced the limits and the hardships, I persist in thinking that our activity is possible, important and necessary.

I wouldn't venture to give lessons, everyone has to find their own way.

All around us we have examples of how an architect in a local context and in the globalized situation can produce works that are full of energy, capable of solving problems and moving people in a more complex, complicated way than ever at a time that requires us to relate to a global world and deal with advanced technologies.

A Constant Turning Point

Conversations between Josep Lluís Mateo and Félix Arranz. Edited by Jaume Prat

The interviews conducted to prepare this publication took place at a turning point in the work of Josep Lluís Mateo. In itself, that is not saying much, since if there is one thing that has characterized the career of Josep Lluís, it is his readiness to constantly investigate, this visible process that is his body of work. The conversations, conducted by Félix Arranz for *scalæ*, took place in and around 2012. I was present for the last two.

This publication sets out to explore everything that underlies the work of Josep Lluís Mateo. The editors step back from the interview. The architect is left on his own to explain himself in a monologue in which particular care has been given to preserving the rhythm and the orality of an indefatigable speaker. The second conversation appears after an initial editing to nuance the text and make it a discourse that covers the principles, processes and situations presented in his work. Which does not suffice without reference to that which has no name or explanation, to that breaking of the rule that we call 'everything else'. What you have in your hands is the result of re-editing the work published in 2013 to rewrite and condense the nuances into their current brief form. Seen from a temporal distance, the most valuable part of this text is the realization that his words did not fall short. The turning points he pronounced took place. Josep Lluís continues to reinvent himself. Today we present this text at a new turning point.

BLACK

Black is the non-colour. There is something of pure abstraction about it, zero reflection, non-light. But the colour I like more than black is charcoal grey. It is 80 per cent black with a touch of white. It's a kind of union of opposites. It's got a bit of red. It has greater complexity than black, which is totally impervious. Charcoal grey is black with something else, and I've often used it. It is still abstract, but it has more nuances, more depths. It's not so hard. It can be shiny and smooth. Black is too direct. White is bittersweet. Charcoal grey is a good metaphor. Two antithetical concepts and red. Red gives it fire and blood amid the death, the starvation, the lack of movement of black. Red gives it life. Red has to do with the earth. You dig a hole and it's there when there's clay. Red is earth, more than fire. It is the vital underlying energy in matter, the magma inside a volcano. It is a starting point. Like the primitive world, like everything that has to do with architecture. All of this is related with the basic moments of nature, the cosmos, light, water. What we architects do is something basic: when we build a roof, it is a shelter, something that protects you from the water, a topography. My work is not simply a personal, artistic exercise; it is like writing with a kind of mortar ... the relation with the earth, with the water, with the sun. Something that gives meaning to construction. The primitive is an argument.

SOUL

I would love to build a space that didn't have a predetermined function. I would love to take on projects where precise needs and functions are not the most important thing. Projects where we could experience space, divinity, interior, material. It might sound a bit metaphysical and a bit ridiculous, but a space – something that moves you, that you notice is alive – has to have character, soul.

The buildings that introduced me to architecture, like the Pantheon in Rome – the one that has made the biggest impression on me as a spatial, vital experience – have soul. The case of the Pantheon is a combination of space and light – which is practically all there is, a tectonics that vibrates with light and air – and the use, which is absolutely commonplace. It's wide open; air and water come in, it's full of birds that shit everywhere. It is the intensity of the ruin, of the Piranesian image. It is the past, the present; it's that kind of moment that is at once transcendent and highly commonplace. It is something both ephemeral and eternal.

I am analytical rather than plastic, intellectual rather than manual. They tell me – as something positive – that I see my own work as an intellectual issue, separate from me. And it's true. Years ago I saw a building of mine as a treatise on mathematics: geometric problems that prompted me to lay the floor one way or another. I've always had a tendency to see my work as a result of intellectual analysis, requiring distance. I make an appearance but I'm not there. This is not the attitude of the typical passionate artist.

TIME

I have a bad relationship with my buildings. I try not to see them again. The building is a moment in our history, and it does not belong to us. We are intermediaries. When we finish, the building begins – we hand it over to the client and disappear. Until that moment, more or less, we might believe that the building belongs to us. And to some extent, that's how it is. I'm very aware of this. When I finish, I say goodbye. The painters are putting the finishing touches to it. It's not clean, but you can see it. That is the moment when the building is mine. It is important so that you don't suffer, you don't see the dramas, great and small, the errors, which are very painful, the savagery, the lack of appreciation on the part of the users, the misinterpretation of the instructions of use ...

Architecture is tough. Although it aims to be pragmatic and helpful, it proposes changes. Real changes. You see this when you finish a building. The reaction upon entering is sometimes that of being attacked. Architecture is unequivocal, precise ... It states one thing and ceases to be everything else.

Ageing is a fact I've never taken much into account. Time is in the project. I'm not very good at living historicity in my work. I perceive it, but in a less linear way than a critic might. That's why I'm not a critic. The critic highlights the temporality of things. The zero moment, that of the origin. For someone on the inside, this position is absolutely impossible. I am taut between the projects before and afterwards. Now doesn't exist. The first works went unnoticed and later they were celebrated all the more so, like Ullastret, which was an important one for me, and people constantly ask to publish it as though it were a present-day project. Past, present and future interact in us.

IN – OUT

I've always considered myself a European architect. With my own specific roots, of course, but moving around a common place between north and south, between Protestant rigour and Catholic permissiveness. My ongoing professional and academic practice in this context simply confirms this determination. And it is not just determination; the ultimate essence of my work is cosmopolitan without relinquishing the specific. This forces you to broaden your horizons, to suspend judgement, to extend your understanding of the other, who is also you, and to bring an open, unbiased approach to the project.

But, underneath it all, architecture is local. I am increasingly aware of my relationship with my roots. My mother was Valencian: the sea, *Cañas y Barro*,[1] the local culture, a certain Mediterranean sensuality ... But I like metal. Cast metal, which uses heat, is fine work. You can mould it. It represents that kind of brutal energy it contains within. I like fire. It is magical, liquid ... and, almost by definition, it needs precision. Any blacksmith, anywhere, needs true 1:1 plans. I like to think about where the joins will go. My big moment is insisting down to the last millimetre to see where the cut needs to be made.

My best projects seek me out. Of course, I look for them, too, but if they arrive it's because they want to arrive.

---

1. *Cañas y Barro* is a novel by Vicent Blasco Ibáñez, written in 1902, and set in the rural periphery of Valencia.

MAGIC REALISM

The commonplace is a very interesting and attractive theme. We operate within the commonplace. The commonplace is thin. It is a form that we do not re-examine, that we find and are not moved by. It refers to things that are devalued, that had meaning, thickness, value, and that come to us as remnants. We operate with conventions. The interest of our work lies in working and changing them, or distorting them. I'm interested in the commonplace not as a prejudice, but, sometimes, as a starting point.

I've always had a curious relationship with success and failure. It seems to me that success is the run-up to failure. When you reach the peak, you have to come down. On my long-distance path of survival, I try to advance rather than triumph.

My work aims to be subtle; complex, precise and subtle. One day Alejandro Zaera said about my Amsterdam dwellings that they were magical. That's a powerful adjective; I like it. They are obviously solid, earthy dwellings, but they possess air. I like the idea that the architect is like a magician, pulling rabbits out of a hat – that is, defining an expected but non-existent product, which produces an unusual but necessary result. The architect as a pragmatic, efficient professional with no soul, no magic, does not interest me at all.

NUANCES: THICKNESS

I've always been a dissident. What I dislike about contemporary architecture is its lack of discourse regarding material. It is a form implemented without attention to physicality. It is a mass that seems to have turned up any old how. I try to define material. From the perspective of feeling like an international architect, this kind of close, concrete materialization is an argument of local culture.

    I tend to imagine things as thick. Thickness is related to mass. Thickness allows us to understand the final layer in relation to all the others.

NUANCES: OPTIMISM

The challenge of continuing to operate as an architect in a rapidly changing world like ours is very attractive. My point of view is a bit special. On the one hand, the role that I like to follow has permanent parts (the artisan encounters, which I was not fully aware of before; now I see that the material quality of things is special).

The 'what' and the 'how' are linked. An idea can be had in seconds. And you can get caught up for years doing it. Which is not trivial. Michelangelo said that the transition from the idea to the work is made on your knees, and when you have completed it, and you're exhausted, it has to appear frivolous. The work has to appear as the whim of the moment.